Round Up The Usual Subjects

Thoughts On Just About Everything

Robert Brault

Round Up The Usual Subjects © 2014 by Robert Brault.

Robert Brault is a Connecticut free-lance writer who has contributed to newspapers and periodicals in the USA since 1961. His work appears in many published anthologies and has been quoted widely on the internet

Robert Brault is quoted several hundred times each day on Twitter. These quotes comprise a realtime stream viewable by linking to **http://twitter.com/search?q=Robert% 20Brault&src=tyah&f=realtime.**

This book may be purchased at the author's website, **rbrault. blogspot.com** or by contacting him at email address, **bobbrault@att.net**.

Front Cover: "Bridge in Fall", watercolor by Joan Brault

ISBN-13: 978-1499593785
ISBN-10: 1499593783

Author's Note

I want to underscore the fact that all writings in this book are original.

Some items will ring familiar, having been in public circulation for years. A number have appeared in *Reader's Digest,* dozens more in other publications and venues, ranging from the CBS TV series *Criminal Minds* to the Ivory Soap wrapper.

I've been pleased to see my thoughts appear on novelty items of all kinds and on more than a million internet sites. One or another of my items is quoted on Twitter about every seven minutes.

It is difficult, indeed impossible, to protect one's creative rights to short writings such as these. I am accustomed to seeing my items credited to others, often to the famous. This book is a hopeful attempt to lay claim to some part of my work. That said, I do encourage the non-commercial use of my items, asking only attribution. I expect that commercial users will contact me for permission.

Robert Brault
bobbrault@att.net

Table of
Contents

~~~

Enjoy the little things, for one day you may look back and realize they were the big things.

~~~

Preface

In 1961, while in college, I sold a Picturesque Speech item to *Reader's Digest*. So began an avocation that has endured to this day. For the next thirty years, I programmed computers by day and wrote aphorisms by night. Some 1200 items made it into magazines and newspapers between 1961 and 1994.

In 2009, seven years into retirement (and after a fifteen-year respite from writing), I launched an internet blog, called *A Robert Brault Reader*. My hope was to find a new audience for my published writings. To my surprise, the effort reawakened the old muse, and new thoughts began to flow.

The blog was noticed by Terri Guillemets at *The Quote Garden,* the internet's most popular quote site. She soon was showcasing some 400 of my items, each with a hyperlink back to my site. Soon thereafter, a Google search would routinely turn up a million sites quoting my items. Today, although I blog only occasionally, I find myself quoted on Twitter several hundred times each day.

This book is a selection of quotes from the blog, peppered here and there with a bit of verse. The quotes are presented by topic, the topics arranged in alphabetical order. My hope is that the book will serve as both a quick reference and an entertaining bedside browse.

I have indeed selected the quotes with an eye toward entertainment. You will find little preaching here and no political commentary (save a few potshots on the foibles of politicians generally.) There is no religious advocacy, although my thoughts are strongly sympathetic to those who find a need for God in their lives.

The thoughts, for the most part, are geared to tried and true virtues -- to faith, hope and charity, to pluck and optimism, to tolerance , compassion and understanding. Mixed in, you will find a healthy dollop of the wry, the sly and the facetious, but you will find no malice.

Will you find wisdom in these pages? Yes, but only the wisdom you bring to them. My goal is to put into words that which we all know full well but seldom express. The deal, as I tell my blog readers, is that I supply the words, you supply the insight.

That said, I do hope you enjoy the book.

Robert Brault

Acknowledgments

My thanks to Terri Guillemets, founder and proprietor of *The Quote Garden* (quotegarden. com), whose sponsorship of my blog was a key factor in its success.

Thanks also to all my blog readers, most especially to those who regularly left comments or sent encouraging emails. You know who you are (and so do I.)

And deepest thanks to Joan Brault, my wife, partner and soulmate, who diligently proofread this book and whose artwork graces the front cover.

~~~

There is nothing instructive in a wise saying. It does not impart to you a skill; it does not provide you new information. It is education in the purest sense -- a drawing out of what has been latent in your understanding. Your pleasure in the saying does not come from having learned something but from having something you knew elucidated and confirmed. What we call wisdom is the expression of what we already know in our hearts.

~~~

Action

Keynote Thought

Everything happens for the purpose of what you decide to do about it.

~~~

Observations

Never act until you have clearly answered the question, "What happens if I do nothing?"

~~~

Right now, before you do it, is the time to ask what you might have done differently.

~~~

There is no such thing as a list of reasons. There is either one sufficient reason or a list of excuses.

~~~

Action

You will never find a reason good enough by adding together reasons that aren't.

~~~

The trouble with leaving yourself a way out is that you always take it.

~~~

The danger in life is that we will keep going nowhere because we know the way.

~~~

If You Want My Advice

Do not hesitate to take the blame, for it puts the blame where you can do something about it.

~~~

No matter what you hear said about yourself, do what you would do if you hadn't heard it.

~~~

Always list things to do in doable order.

~~~

Voice of Experience

The most basic strategy is to get time on your side. The most basic tactic is to sit and wait.

~~~

Dry, Sly and Wry

When everything worth doing has been done, there will be plenty worth undoing.

~~~

Life is a series of tasks that absolutely must get done before they don't matter any more.

~~~

And a Reminder

If you haven't time to respond to a tug at your pants leg, your schedule is too crowded.

~~~

See also Perseverance, Success

Adversity

Nature decrees that we do not exceed the speed of light. All other impossibilities are optional.

~ ~ ~

Observations

You can bear your troubles or shrug them off. They're your shoulders.

~~~

Sometimes what seems like an impossible climb is just a staircase without the steps drawn in.

~~~

There is a lesson in every failure, for those who remember the lesson and forget the failure.

~~~

Where the loser saw barriers, the winner saw hurdles.

Occasionally it's good to retrace our footsteps --
to remind ourselves who made them.

~~~

Opportunity is never a shiny new coin. It is a
much-circulated coin, many times ill-spent,
seeking hands that will spend it to purpose.

~~~

<u>If You Want My Advice</u>

Never mind the odds against you. If you double
your effort, what will the odds against you do --
send for reinforcements?

~~~

<u>Dry, Sly and Wry</u>

Some days are such perfect disasters that there's
nothing to do but sit back and admire their
perfection.

~~~

Aging

You're never too old, but you're always too young to know it.

~~~

Observations

It is possible at any age to discover a lifelong desire you never knew you had.

~~~

Never use the passing years as an excuse for old age.

~~~

It is never too late, especially when it would otherwise be too late.

~~~

How True, How True.

You get to an age when no matter what happens, you wish someone would put a stop to it.

~~~~

Say what you want about aging, it's still the only way to have old friends.

~~~

While it's romantic to talk about growing old together, it mostly happens while you're napping.

~~~

You spend the first two-thirds of your life asking to be left alone and the last third not having to ask.

~~~

What you notice as the years go by is that your friends keep getting older and strangers keep getting younger.

~~~

Aging

Speaking For Myself

*I complain of the passing years, but then I look
in a mirror and realize that very few of them
actually got past.*

~~~

*In this, the late afternoon of my life, I wonder:
"Am I casting a longer shadow, or is my shadow
casting a shorter me?"*

~~~

*Having nearly completed the book of life, I can
tell you that the answers are not in the back.*

~~~

Metaphor, Anyone?

*Father Time keeps pitching the years at us. We
swing and miss at a few. We hit a few out of the
park. We try not to take any called strikes.*

~~~

See also Retirement

Animals

Keynote Thought

The only animal whose native habitat is a zoo is the zookeeper.

~~~

Speaking For Myself

I believe in animal rights, and high among them is the right to the gentle stroke of a human hand.

~~~

If we don't feel a bond with the animals who share with us this moment in eternity, we don't comprehend eternity.

~~~

There is in every animal a sense of duty that man condescends to call instinct.

~~~

Dry, Sly and Wry

Man is rated the highest animal, at least among the animals who returned the questionnaire.

~~~

If a rabbit defined intelligence the way man does, then the most intelligent animal would be a rabbit, followed by the animal most willing to obey the commands of a rabbit.

~~~

For the most part, we carnivores do not eat other carnivores. We prefer to eat our vegetarian friends.

~~~

Only man can behold a lion and think that he, man, is the one made in God's image.

~~~

Man is the only trained animal who expects his reward before he does his trick.

~~~

The smarter the animal, the better it is at pretending to be trained.

Man is the only animal who enjoys the consolation of believing in a next life. All other animals enjoy the consolation of not worrying about it.

~~~

Grist For The Thought Mill

It is a perversely human perception that animals in their native habitat are running wild.

~~~

If man were relieved of all superstition, and all prejudice, and had replaced these with a keen sensitivity to his real environment, and moreover had achieved a level of communication so simplified that one syllable could express his every desire, then he would have achieved the level of intelligence already achieved by his dog.

~~~

See Also Pets

Apology

Keynote Thought

Life becomes easier when you learn to accept an apology you never got.

~~~

Observations

An important thing to get to know about a person is the unspoken ways they say they're sorry.

~~~

You don't have to be the one at fault to be the one who's sorry.

~~~

Sometimes we regret, more than any words spoken, a silence not broken.

~~~

For every person who atones, there are a hundred who find regret sufficient.

~~~

You learn this about apologizing, "I'm sorry <u>that</u>" is a better start than "I'm sorry <u>if</u>."

~~~

If You Want My Advice

When someone says, "I'm sorry if you took offense," say to them, "Come back when you're sorry you gave it."

~~~

Art and Artists

Keynote Thought

It is easier to reach perfection than to stop there.

~~~

Observations

Every great painting is left incomplete at the point where its completion is obvious.

~~~

There is in art the notion that less is more, which is to say, you don't torture a painting that has already confessed.

~~~

Art is an innate distrust of the theory of reality concocted by the five senses.

~~~

Sometimes, to pursue a new idea, the artist must forfeit his deposit on an old idea.

~~~

The artist puts brush to canvas, and the poet puts pen to paper. The poet has the easier task, for his pen does not alter his rhyme.

~~~

What you see, often, in a lesser work of art is a subject perfectly captured but never set free.

~~~

<u>Dry, Sly and Wry</u>

The artist wonders, "Have I barely scratched the surface of my talent, or is scratching a surface all the talent I have?"

~~~

The artist uses the talent he has, wishing he had more talent. The talent uses the artist it has, wishing it had more artist.

~~~

Art and Artists

An artist must marry his talent -- and the two must elope. A big church wedding is fatal.

~~~

A painting is what you make of it, besides which "Moon Weeping" has a better ring to it than "Paintbrush Dripping."

~~~

The first assumption of an art critic is that the artist meant to paint something else.

~~~

An art critic is someone who appreciates art except for any particular piece of art.

~~~

To the artist, Genesis is a tale of six days in which God suggested some really good ideas.

~~~

Oh, how much simpler
Things would be,
If eyes could paint
Or brush could see.

~~~

Create Your Own Aphorism

There is in every artist's studio a scrap heap of discarded works in which the artist's [select from list] *prevailed against his* [select from list].

Selections:

hand
eye
brush
imagination
daring
discipline
talent
other

Example:

There is in every artist's studio a scrap heap of discarded works in which the artist's discipline prevailed against his daring.

~~~

Attitude

There are exactly as many special occasions in life as we choose to celebrate.

~~~

Observations

If you can be unaccountably sad, you can be unaccountably happy.

~~~

Things happen to justify whatever mood you're in.

~~~

Two people can have a middling day, but one rounds up and the other rounds down.

~~~

If you can wear the hard times of your life as furrows on your brow, you can wear the good times as a twinkle in your eye.

~~~

If You Want My Advice

Refuse to be burdened by vague worries. If something wants to worry you, insist that it make itself clear.

~~~

Before you call any work menial, watch a proud person do it.

~~~

Speaking For Myself

We find things where we look for them, which is why I never look for a golf ball out of bounds.

~~~

Be Yourself

Keynote Thought

*We all have our limitations, but when we listen
to our critics, we also have theirs.*

~~~

Observations

*There is a limit to how much you can change to
be liked for who you really are.*

~~~

*You can try to be someone else, but it's easier to
just be yourself and apologize as necessary.*

~~~

*It's important to be your own friend, especially
on days when you wouldn't care to make your
own acquaintance.*

~~~

Every temptation to follow the crowd is an opportunity to be thankful you didn't.

~~~

What you discover about people you try not to offend is that you can offend them without trying.

~~~

If you allow people to treat you like a doormat, they will expect you to say WELCOME.

~~~

Walking The Walk

Looking back, you realize that a very special person passed briefly through your life, and that person was you. It is not too late to become that person again.

~~~

In public, I am who others need me to be. In private, I am who I need me to be. Who am I really? Doesn't matter. Not needed.

~~~

If You Want My Advice

*Never mind searching for who you are. Search
for the person you aspire to be.*

~~~

*Always laugh off a slight insult, so that people
will know what it means when you're not
laughing.*

~~~

*Do what you must,
And your friends will adjust.*

~~~

*Do not look to find your identity in some
particular work. Look to stamp your identity
on whatever work you do.*

~~~

*Why try to be someone you're not? Life is tough
enough without adding impersonation to the
skills required.*

~~~

Dry, Sly And Wry

Know thyself, for it greatly lessens the danger that you will accidentally reveal it to someone else.

~~~

Know thyself, especially thyself after a couple of drinks.

~~~

It's annoying to be disapproved of by people who know only half the story, especially when you're not sure which half they know.

~~~

If you can't figure out who you are, you might as well work on who you want to be.

~~~

The most important thing to know about yourself is where you usually leave your car keys.

~~~

So it turns out that all those years they were calling you a dim bulb, they meant you were efficient.

~~~

Speaking For Myself

If God had intended me to make excuses for who I am, He would have given me better excuses.

~~~

I am told to just be myself, but as much as I have practiced the impression, I'm still no good at it.

~~~

Every day I go forth to seek my identity, feeling greatly blessed by the things I don't find it in.

~~~

Long ago I discovered the real me. The meeting was cordial, the decision to part mutual, and we remain friends.

~~~

Beauty

To be loved is to be beautiful in someone's eyes, and when you think about it, is there any other way to be beautiful?

~~~

Observations

We ask, "What do they see in each other?" when the question should be, "What do they choose to overlook?"

~~~

The secret to being beautiful is to find someone who thinks you are and let them convince you.

~~~

Inner beauty, too, needs occasionally to be told it is beautiful.

~~~

Beauty

It is a rare woman who can overcome her desire to remain pretty and allow herself to become beautiful.

~~~

We try to preserve our attractiveness by disguising our age and end up revealing our age by disguising our attractiveness.

~~~

There is no actual law that says a person of inner beauty cannot also maintain an appearance.

~~~

<u>Dry, Sly and Wry</u>

No one ever became a scintillating conversationalist who had the option of just standing there, looking great.

~~~

Ever wonder how a hotel bathroom mirror knows what you will look like in twenty years?

~~~

Belief

Keynote Thought

Sometimes you believe a thing that isn't true because in the world you wish to live in, it would be true.

~~~

Observations

An old belief is like an old shoe -- we so value its comfort that we fail to notice the hole in it.

~~~

It is hard to challenge a belief that people do not insist be true

~~~

It's just crazy not to believe in the miracles your happiness depends on.

~~~

Belief

The difference between truth and belief is that belief is not always on your side.

~~~

If You Want My Advice

Beware a belief that has long withstood the test of not being challenged.

~~~

Speaking For Myself

A rule I try to follow is this: Never believe anything that requires you to hate people who do not believe it.

~~~

I believe there is an explanation for everything, so, yes, I believe in miracles.

~~~

Charity

Keynote Thought

The willingness to share does not make one charitable, it makes one free.

~~~

Observations

Delay never made a kindness any kinder.

~~~

There's a lot of selfishness that goes by the name of minding your own business.

~~~

There is no charity less costly to bestow and more genuinely appreciated than a small compliment.

~~~

To suppress a hurtful truth is also charity.

Charity

If You Want My Advice

Never say to someone in need, "You know where to reach me."   Notice, instead, that they have already reached you.

~~~

Act always from a sense of common humanity, and let others decide if it be charity.

~~~

Words Of My Mother

"Helping someone in need is not charity, it is proper etiquette."

~~~

Walking The Walk

Today I bent the truth to be kind, and I have no regret, for I am far surer of what is kind than I am of what is true.

~~~

Childhood

Keynote Thought

If you can recall what the world was like when you were a wide-eyed kid, then you know what the world is like right now.

~~~

Observations

To trade a childhood wonder for a plausible explanation -- is there a worse trade we make in life?

~~~

The thing most missed from childhood days is the ability to enjoy happiness while it is still in progress.

~~~

For every childhood question there is a preposterous answer that you weren't actually supposed to believe forever.

The Fiction of Childhood

It is not just the fiction of Santa Claus -- or the Easter Bunny or the Tooth Fairy -- we create for our kids but the fiction of childhood itself. It extends to summer evenings chasing fireflies and picnics by the lake, a make-believe world made possible by the illusion that Dad and Mom are in charge and there is nothing to fear.

~~~

In childhood we press our nose to the pane, looking out. In memories of childhood, we press our nose to the pane, looking in.

~~~

See also Kids, Parenting

Choice

Keynote Thought

*To be bound by our choices is not to have lost
our freedom but to have exercised it.*

~~~

Observations

*So often we choose to continue the life we know
only to discover that it was not one of the
choices.*

~~~

*They who avoid the tough choices of life live a
life they never chose.*

~~~

*Freedom is a ticket to ride, of no value if you
never choose to go anywhere.*

~~~

Choice

How True, How True

Life is a series of choices, all made at too young an age.

~~~

The trouble with making a choice is that something always happens afterwards, and you think you chose it.

~~~

Speaking For Myself

I choose to awaken not to an array of choices but to a clear duty born of the choices I have made.

~~~

I have made my choices. I carry them as snapshots in my wallet.

~~~

Cosmic Understanding

Keynote Thought

I would rather be me and have to explain the universe than be the universe and have to explain me.

~~~

Observations

The thing missing in man's quest to understand the universe is someone else's point of view.

~~~

In man's study of the cosmos, there has never been a mystery that a larger mystery would not explain.

~~~

Although man has found many pieces to the universal jigsaw puzzle, he has yet to find a side piece.

~~~

Grist For The Thought Mill

When you've tried all your life to solve a mystery and failed, you must consider the possibility that it is not a mystery.

~~~

One day, there will be only one thing left to understand, and when we come to understand it, it will change our understanding of everything else.

~~~

Speaking For Myself

My quest for cosmic understanding is a book I have picked up and put down many times, each time failing to insert a bookmark.

~~~

It is my luck that every time I feel I comprehend God's plan, I don't have a pencil with me.

~~~

I've always thought that the vastness of the night sky is an incredible example of what can be done with mirrors, assuming that's the way it was done.

~~~

Dry, Sly and Wry

What we know about the universe is that it began as a swirling pool of gas that, as it cooled, spun off the Ten Commandments.

~~~

Metaphor, Anyone?

Night sky: a trillion asterisks and no explanations.

~~~

See also Faith, God

Destiny

Any intersection can be the corner of Destiny and Chance, any barroom the Karma Lounge of the Serendipity Hotel.

~~~

Observations

Every believer in chance is just once chance meeting away from believing in destiny.

~~~

It is sad when two people turn from the paths they're traveling, and their paths go on to cross without them.

~~~

Sometimes in life you have an appointment with destiny, and sometimes you just have to get destiny to squeeze you in.

~~~

Speaking For Myself

Seems like every time I go to the ocean, the tide comes in when I want it to go out, the sort of luck that has dogged me all my life.

~~~

Alas, by the time Fate caught up to my life, Chance had it all planned.

~~~

Metaphor, Anyone?

Two raindrops, flung from the heavens, merge on a windowpane. Chance meeting? Tell it to the two raindrops.

~~~

Last I heard from my destiny, it wanted me to go one-quarter mile and make a legal U-turn.

~~~

Driving

Keynote Thought

An object at rest tends to stay at rest, especially if you're behind it when the light turns green.

~~~

Dry, Sly and Wry

*Road sign that most applies to life itself:
EXPECT DELAYS.*

~~~

A commuter tie-up consists of you and people who for some reason won't use public transit.

~~~

Road rage is the expression of the amateur sociopath in all of us, cured by running into a professional.

~~~

It finally happened. I got the GPS lady so confused that she said, "In one-quarter mile, make a legal stop and ask directions."

~~~

"And I, I took the road less traveled by" -- I was using a GPS system.

~~~

For every sign that says "Drive Carefully," shouldn't there be a sign that says, "Resume Normal Driving?"

~~~

<u>Words Most Likely To Be Spoken By Someone In The Passenger's Seat Looking Up From Her Knitting</u>

"Wasn't that our exit?"

~~~

Education

Keynote Thought

The word "education" comes from the word "educe," which means to "draw out." So much of teaching is the opposite, a "pounding in" of facts, rules and methods. But there are moments magical to a teacher, moments of true education, when the teacher engages a child's cognition -- and finds recognition.

~~~

The average teacher explains complexity. The gifted teacher reveals simplicity.

~~~

Though it invariably meets the requirements of the school board, education is not merely the extension of ignorance to every subject in the approved curriculum.

~~~

Too often the first thing a child learns in school is to stop asking questions that can't be answered.

~~~

<u>Dry, Sly and Wry</u>

The difference between education and know-how is that one you pay for, the other you charge for.

~~~

It's reported that ignorance of math is growing by geometric progression, whatever that is.

~~~

Emotions

Never let your emotions rule, but always let them testify.

~~~

Observations

It is a safe bet that anyone who tells you you need to calm down has never actually seen you when you needed to calm down.

~~~

Moral outrage is better worn up your sleeve than on your sleeve.

~~~

In people who change the world, there is a calm that is the storm.

~~~

One thing you never want to lose in life is your capacity to be quietly appalled.

~~~

Speaking For Myself

Why do I let my emotions get the better of me? For the same reason I let it rain last Tuesday.

~~~

I assume, when the Lord assigns credit for loving thy neighbor, He will count crying at movies.

~~~

Entitlement

Keynote Thought

Nothing we feel entitled to ever comes to us in sufficient abundance to make us happy.

~~~

Observations

Shall you redirect your life's journey because down some side road is some trifle you're entitled to?

~~~

What we earn by the sweat of our brow, we defend with pride. What we gain by the accident of birth, we guard with prejudice.

~~~

Beware a politician who claims to know what you deserve.

~~~

If You Want My Advice

Never trust to luck, unless you know what it would be a reward for.

~~~

Speaking For Myself

Am I some ant that I should drop what I have gathered to chase every crumb in my path?

~~~

Dry, Sly and Wry

To err is human, to forgive does not get you the settlement that we at Susskind, Marberry and Callahan feel you're entitled to.

~~~

Faith

Keynote Thought

*It is not unreasonable to have faith in that
which is necessary for your happiness.*

~~~

Observations

*If you listed all the reasons for your faith, and
all the things that make you cry, it would be
essentially the same list.*

~~~

*To some, that which cannot be explained is a
mystery. To others, that which cannot be
explained is the explanation.*

~~~

*What is certainty but the refuge of those whose
faith is not strong enough to entertain doubt.*

~~~

Speaking For Myself

I was once a skeptic but was converted by the two missionaries on either side of my nose.

~~~

Of course I doubt. I do not practice a certainty. I practice a faith.

~~~

Having long struggled with my doubt, I now struggle with my faith -- a small step forward.

~~~

Some have been to the mountain. I have been to my knees by the side of my bed.

~~~

Dry, Sly and Wry

All we know for certain about the next life is that you arrive there ahead of your luggage.

~~~

See also God

Family

Family life is a bit like a runny peach pie, not perfect but who's complaining?

~~~

Observations

To say that a family is bound by blood is to underestimate the adhesive power of sweat and tears.

~~~

I have never known a family activity so trivial that it didn't take my mind off something less important.

~~~

The thing about family disasters is that you never have to wait long before the next one puts the previous one into perspective.

~~~

In bringing up kids, there is no daily chore so slight that it cannot be made critical by skipping it two days running.

~~~

A family is a group of people who stick essentially the same nose into each other's business.

~~~

If minutes were kept of a family meeting, "Members Not Present" and "Subjects Discussed" would be one and the same.

~~~

In a household of toddlers and pets, you can start out having a bad day, but you keep getting sidetracked.

~~~

Nothing shakes one's faith in democracy like the family's 3 to 2 vote for fudge sundaes for breakfast.

~~~

How True, How True

The more spill-proof cups, the happier the toast.

~~~

A child never thinks to look for a toy where he last threw it.

~~~

If the older sibling has lost a toy, the younger sibling knows where it is.

~~~

The ideal family board game is one that can be played each time with fewer pieces.

~~~

A common parental fallacy is that a lost Scrabble tile has to be somewhere in the house.

~~~

A family vacation trip is one-third pleasure, fondly remembered, and two-thirds aggravation, entirely forgotten.

~~~

The Family Dictionary

Family: a group of strangers who always sit at the same place at dinner.

Sibling: someone with whom you have nothing in common, frequently mistaken for you.

Cousin: someone you see twice a year, the second time to return the dish.

Great Uncle, Great Aunt:
someone at whose funeral you know you're too close to the casket when people keep telling you they're sorry for your loss.

Family Friend:
someone who, as a kid, you never knew who they were except they always brought the macaroni casserole.

Your Own Apartment:
a place where you can be sick in the bathroom at 1 AM without your mother knocking at the door and asking if you're all right.

See also Parenting

Fitness

The brain forgets much, but the lower back remembers everything.

~~~

Dry, Sly and Wry

The way some people treat their bodies, you'd think they were renting.

~~~

It's one thing to accept who you are, and another thing to appear in public in such a condition.

~~~

After years of buying clothes I intend to diet into, I'll say this: "The skeleton in my closet has some really nice outfits."

~~~

Of all the pretenses of the cocktail party season, the hardest is pretending that your clothes fit.

~~~

Overheard At The Fitness Center

"The last straw was when someone called my daughter a chick off the old blop."

~~~

"I have never photographed well, and lately I'm not reflecting all that well in mirrors."

~~~

"So I said to myself, 'There but for the grace of God go I,' only to realize that I was looking in a mirror and had seriously overestimated the grace of God."

~~~

Forgiveness

Life is too short to hold a grudge, also too long.

~~~

Observations

If you can't forgive and forget, pick one.

~~~

Often what seems like an unforgiving heart is just time that needs to go by.

~~~

To truly forgive is to let the other person forget.

~~~

If every sin were forgivable, there would be no need for forgiveness.

~~~

The beauty of forgiveness is that it requires only a forgiving party. There needn't be a party worthy of forgiveness.

~~~

It is perhaps unfair to ask forgiveness of love, but that is generally the injured party.

~~~

You can build a forgiving relationship on love, but it's harder to build a loving relationship on forgiveness.

~~~

To say, "I love you. Why would I hurt you?" is to ask not for forgiveness but for psychoanalysis.

~~~

It can be easier to forgive when you remember that you are not God and your forgiveness does not confer absolution.

~~~

Friendship

Keynote Thought

Do not be someone looking for friendship. Be friendship looking for someone.

~~~

Observations

It is a good friend who tells you a harsh truth, wanting ten times more to tell you a loving lie.

~~~

It's sad to see a friendship expire because you carelessly assumed that it would automatically renew.

~~~

You always think you could have done more, which is why you need a friend -- to tell you you did all you could.

~~~

Most of us don't need a psychoanalyst as much as a friend to be silly with.

~~~

When a friend needs consolation, nothing will keep so well until tomorrow as the truth.

~~~

Sometimes it is the person closest to us who must travel the furthest distance to be our friend.

~~~

Eventually we realize that not all opposing viewpoints come from people who oppose us.

~~~

Our most difficult task as a friend is to offer understanding when we don't understand.

~~~

It is a true friend who asks, "Is there anything I can do to help?", knowing there is.

~~~

Friendship

There are people who, if given the chance, would do you harm, which is why it's good to hang out with people who have already had the chance.

~~~

No matter how sure you are that a friend will be there for you, it's still the greatest feeling when the time comes, and there they are.

~~~

The thing you notice about people with lots of friends is that they don't require a membership.

~~~

It's hard to be best friend to someone who won't let you be best at anything else.

~~~

The best marriages are between two who seek the same God, the best friendships between two who flee the same devil.

~~~

If You Want My Advice

Today, befriend a stranger, or if you feel up to more of a challenge, befriend a loved one.

~~~

Speaking For Myself

I like friends who, when you tell them you need a moment alone, know enough not to stray too far.

~~

I value the friend who for me finds time on his calendar, but I cherish the friend who for me does not consult his calendar.

~~~

Wry, Sly and Dry

We all play the leading role in our own situation comedy, but occasionally it's fun to play the goofy friend in somebody else's.

~~~

Gardening

Overnight it rained, and the wind shifted into the west, and this morning my garden is fresh in the sun, and its scent wafts through my window. But if I sit in my garden, who will keep my appointment in town? But if I keep my appointment in town, who will sit in my garden?

~~~

Observations

Why try to explain miracles to your kids when you can just have them plant a garden?

~~~

In every gardener there is a child who believes in The Seed Fairy.

~~~

A child's garden is a triumph of hope over too much watering.

~~~

What is a gardener but a magician's assistant?

~~~

If you've never experienced the thrill of accomplishing more than you can imagine, plant a garden.

~~~

There is no logical path that begins with a packet of seeds and ends in despair.

~~~

Gardening

It is not known whether flowers really can't talk or just exercise unfailingly good judgment in the matter.

~~~

Speaking For Myself

It pleases me to take amateur photographs of my garden, and it pleases my garden to make my photographs look professional.

~~~

I sit in my garden, gazing upon a beauty that cannot gaze upon itself, and I find sufficient purpose for my day.

~~~

As a gardener, I am among those who believe that much of the evidence of God's existence has been planted.

~~~

I cultivate my garden, and my garden cultivates me.

~~~

God

Keynote Thought

In many areas of understanding, none so much as in our understanding of God, we bump up against a simplicity so profound that we must assign complexities to it to comprehend it at all. It is mindful of how we paste decals to a sliding glass door to keep from bumping our nose against it.

~~~

Observations

God answers first the prayers we should have prayed.

~~~

In nature we see where God has been. In our fellow man, we see where He is still at work.

~~~

God

Though we sometimes wonder why God does what He does, we can be sure He does it on better information.

~~~

If God had wanted to be a big secret, He would not have created babbling brooks and whispering pines.

~~~

The most compelling argument that God exists is that the job position so clearly exists.

~~~

Sometimes, as practice for convincing myself that God exists, I try to convince my shadow that the sun exists.

~~~

Even if you think the Big Bang created the universe, don't you wonder who sent the flowers?

~~~

See also Cosmic Understanding, Faith

Gramps and Granny

Keynote Thought

Becoming a grandparent is one of the few pleasures in life for which the consequences have already been paid.

~~~

Observations

To a small child, a granddad is someone unafraid of big dogs and fierce storms but absolutely terrified of the word, "boo!"

~~~

What does a woman wish to be, who, finding at her door a small figure with a tiny suitcase, does not wish to be Grandmother?

~~~

Speaking For Myself

I would gladly go back and travel the road not taken, if I knew at the end of it I'd find the same set of grandkids.

~~~

A Recollection

I remember one Christmas being told that there was no Santa Claus, and the next Easter being told that there was no Easter Bunny, and I remember, as Thanksgiving approached, how I feared that they would tell me there was no Grandmother.

~~~

Gratitude

Keynote Thought

*There is no such thing as gratitude unexpressed.
If it is unexpressed, it is plain old-fashioned
ingratitude.*

~~

Observations

*Any occasion that requires a gift requires an
enthusiastic appreciation of the gift.*

~~~

*It takes a while, but eventually we realize that the
people who were always there for the special
occasions of our youth had other things to do.*

~~~

*Always invite into your success the friends who
helped you get there, for they are the ones most
likely to wait for an invitation.*

~~~

Grieving

*Sometimes in tragedy we find our life's purpose,
the eye sheds a tear to find its focus.*

~~~

Observations

*We grieve because we care, and with the
passage of time, our consolation is knowing that
we cared.*

~~~

*In the end, the reason for anything is
inseparable from the reason for everything.*

~~~

*It is not until you lose someone you loved too
much that you realize you didn't love them too
much enough.*

~~~

Every day is conquerable by its hours and every hour by its minutes.

~~~

A senseless tragedy remains forever tragic, but it's up to us whether it remains forever senseless.

~~~

Yes, people we love die. But it's either that or people dying unloved.

~~~

There comes a time when something you loved no longer is, and what sustains you is knowing that there will never come a time when it no longer was.

~~~

Speaking For Myself

As my dying request, I would ask that my loved ones skip the first four stages of grief and go directly to acceptance.

~~~

Growing Apart

Keynote Thought

So often we don't know what we want, and we blame our unhappiness on someone who doesn't know, either.

~~~

Observations

For want of an occasional expression of love, a relationship strong at the seams can wear thin in the middle.

~~~

*Sometimes two people
need to step apart
and make a space between
that each might see the other anew
in a glance across a room
or silhouetted against the moon.*

~~~

It is so hard to realize that a good thing will never be a better thing and still let it be a good thing.

~~~

A lovers' quarrel is always about every quarrel you ever had.

~~~

It can be a lifelong battle to love someone through the chinks in their armor.

~~

Sometimes just the right degree of separation makes the most lasting bond.

~~~

One of life's curious puzzles is how two people can travel the same road to two different places.

~~~

So often our greatest triumph is a willing surrender.

~~~

Growing Apart

What good is love if you never ask anything of it?

~~~

You can accept a falling out that changes your plans, but it is hard to accept a betrayal that changes your memories.

~~~

You can as easily love without trusting as you can hug without embracing.

~~~

It is easier to believe that you were never loved than that such a love could die.

~~~

If love is to end, it must end in indifference. If it ends in hate, it hasn't ended.

~~~

Sometimes two people stay together for the sake of the kids -- two kids who sat under a full moon and pledged to be forever true.

~~~

Halloween

Keynote Thought

There is a child in every one of us who is still a trick-or-treater, looking for a brightly-lit front porch.

~~~

Observations

I don't know if there are real ghosts and goblins, but I know that there are always more trick-or-treaters than neighborhood kids.

~~~

Nothing dispels the rattling of ghosts in the attic like the twittering of goblins on the front porch.

~~~

I don't know that there are haunted houses. I know that there are dark staircases and haunted people.

~~~

Halloween

For every bodiless spirit you encounter, there is a spiritless body you really don't want to run across.

~~~

There are moonlit nights when the dead send their ghosts to haunt us -- and dark misty nights when they come themselves.

~~~

The real ghouls of Halloween sit in darkened houses as trick-or-treaters scurry past.

~~~

Every party is a masquerade party. Even an invitation to come as you are is an invitation to come in your usual disguise.

~~~

Happiness

Keynote Thought

Be happy, and a reason will come along.

~~~

Observations

The trick to being happy is to stop postponing it until such time as you can be happier.

~~~

Once you fix it in your mind that life itself is a gift, you start finding happiness in just about everything.

~~~

The first place to look for happiness is where you left it.

~~~

Happiness

So often the search for happiness takes us down a familiar street to an old address.

~~~

If you search the world for happiness, you will find it in the end, for the world is round and will lead you back to your door.

~~~

Seeking happiness, I passed many a traveler headed in the opposite direction, seeking happiness.

~~~

Whatever you set aside to seek happiness, remember where you put it.

~~~

The secret to happiness is to put the burden of proof on unhappiness.

~~~

You can't postpone sorrow, so why would you postpone happiness?

~~~

One day you just say "To heck with it", and you go looking for trouble, and you find happiness.

~~~

Happiness doesn't need a reason. Motive is sufficient.

~~~

Happiness always thinks it could be happier. Sadness never imagines it could be sadder.

~~~

Do not spend your life seeking security and then wonder why you never found happiness.

~~~

There is no harder thing to give up than the thing that was supposed to make you happy.

~~~

Happiness is life served up with a scoop of acceptance, a topping of tolerance and sprinkles of hope, although chocolate sprinkles also work.

~~~

Happiness

It always seems that we would happier in a faraway place, as if you could hop a plane to a state of mind.

~~~

There are two things to know: Happiness comes at a price, and you have already paid it.

~~~

The ultimate regret is to realize that what you asked of life was never sufficient to make you happy.

~~~

<u>If You Want My Advice</u>

Seek out someone who wants to make you happy and let them.

~~~

Be hopeful and happy, and if it proves unwarranted, apologize to anyone you hurt by it.

~~~

Home and Household

Keynote Thought

We labor to make a house a home, then every time we're expecting guests, we rush to turn it back into a house.

~~~

Observation

Every home has an unorganized kitchen drawer that, if you organized it, you'd need another kitchen drawer.

~~~

Speaking For Myself

At my house, we have a kitchen drawer organized for knives, forks and spoons and a kitchen drawer organized for dead flashlight batteries, broken corkscrews and used birthday candles.

~~~

Honor

Who would not be a little dishonest, if there were such a thing as a little dishonesty.

~~~

Observations

Eventually all the things we acquire by dishonesty are gone, and we are left with only our dishonesty.

~~~

There is an ongoing battle between conscience and self-interest in which, at some point, we have to take sides.

~~~

The one chance to repair a reputation for dishonesty is while you are still the only one who knows about it.

If you hand over your integrity on a silver platter, they will want it on gold.

~~~

It is not that the honest pursuit of one's selfish interests cannot be a social good; it is that if one is selfish, why would one be honest?

~~~

It's curious how so many feel honor-bound to seek revenge when they don't feel honor-bound to do anything else.

~~~

Speaking For Myself

The phrase "Duty, Honor, Country" is redundant to this extent -- that if you attend to duty and honor, you have fully discharged your obligation to country.

~~~

Hope

Though you lose all hope, there is still hope, and it loves to surprise.

~~~

Observations

You might as well hope for the best, since hoping for less doesn't seem to improve the results any.

~~~

Hope is a path through a flowering meadow. One doesn't require that it lead anywhere.

~~~

Where hope would otherwise become hopelessness, it becomes faith.

~~~

Through the darkest night,
morning gently tiptoes,
feeling its way to dawn.

~~~

If You Want My Advice

Toss your dashed hopes not into a trash bin but
into a drawer where you are likely to rummage
some bright morning.

~~~

Dream small that your dreams may come true.
Dream large that you may always have a
dream.

~~~

A Question

If hope and despair were paths to the same
destination, which would you choose?

~~~

See also Optimism

Humankind

The conclusion, "Nobody cares," is always based on an insufficient sampling.

~~~

Observations

We envy others, for we see their lives in broad outline, while forced to live ours in every detail.

~~~

The most fundamental winning formula is to bet on human decency and be patient.

~~~

Eventually you come to realize that most people aren't looking for a fight but for someone to surrender to.

~~~

No two people are alike, but you take three or more, and they're pretty much the same.

~~~

It is not so much that human beings are all the same as that they have the same differences.

~~~

If we could see others as they see themselves, our shyness would soon become compassion.

~~~

The easiest way to meet new people is to just look like someone who is willing to listen.

~~~

The best solution never requires that someone be right and someone else be wrong.

~~~

The most basic courtesy is to accept people for what they pretend to be, even when they pretend badly.

~~~

Humankind

The most deserving cries for help are never heard because they are never uttered.

~~~

No one passes you on the street who was not once beautiful in somebody's eyes.

~~~

The people in your life who don't need an invitation still like to get one.

~~~

How True, How True

There are people who whoop when they sneeze and people who sneeze softly into a tissue, and they are usually seated side-by-side in tourist class.

~~~

We all know someone who's definitely going to heaven -- unless they have to be there on time.

~~~

If You Want My Advice

Never point a finger where you never lent a hand.

~~~

Count no day lost in which you waited your turn, took only your share and sought advantage over no one.

~~~

Dry, Sly and Wry

Don't look at it as my right to privacy. Look at it as your right to mind your own business.

~~~

While I find that I can keep my nose out of other people's business, I do have a curiosity as to their non-business activities.

~~~

While I'm concerned about man's inhumanity to man, I'm more focused right now on man's inhumanity to me personally.

~~~

Humility

There is a quiet, unassuming pride that no misfortune can humble, and it goes by the name of humility

~~~

Observations

Few are humble, for it requires a self-esteem few possess.

~~~

One learns to ignore criticism by first learning to ignore applause.

~~~

To inspire awe in anyone should serve to inspire embarrassment in ourselves.

~~~

Dry, Sly and Wry

I have been humbled by praise, and I have been humbled by whiffing on the first tee, and somehow it's different.

~~~

The first thing to suspect in people who think highly of us is poor judgment.

~~~

Speaking For Myself

It's not that I'm this larger-than-life figure. It's that I've had this smaller-than-I-figured life.

~~~

I make no claim to fame, realizing that it would probably end up in small claims court anyway.

~~~

And as a last request, I have asked for whatever style tombstone will make the mowing easier.

~~~

Judging Others

Always carry with you a little reasonable doubt, should you meet someone who needs to be found innocent.

~~~

Observations

Sometimes the best exercise of good judgment is knowing when to withhold one's better judgment.

~~~

The key to compassion is to realize that everyone you meet is a set of extenuating circumstances.

~~~

Most people are better than we judge, for we do not know the temptations they have overcome.

Sometimes, to make the right judgment, you have to be too involved to be objective.

~~~

If You Want My Advice

Be reluctant to judge a person whose shadow you have never cast.

~~~

Always when judging
Who people are,
Remember to footnote
The words, "So far."

~~~

Dry, Sly and Wry

Never judge people by the rings they dangle from their facial parts, assuming there's anything else to go on.

~~~

Judging Ourselves

Stay out of the court of self-judgment, for there is no presumption of innocence.

~~~

Observations

Life is a game of dominoes in which every domino blames itself.

~~~

There's no need to take the blame for every fool thing that ever happened, and it's too early anyway.

~~~

Life is a series of events that happen in such a way that it seems to be your fault.

~~~

Self-criticism is always an attempt to head off hearing it from someone else, who otherwise would never have given it a thought.

~~~

The preponderance of the evidence stands little chance against the preponderance of wishing it weren't so.

~~~

The thing about letting yourself be victimized is that it's so hard to blame the right person.

~~~

Speaking For Myself

The verdict is still out on my life, the judge having not yet instructed the jury, both of whom are me.

~~~

Kids

The world is as many times new as there are children in our lives.

~~~

Observations

A child seldom needs a good talking-to as much as a good listening-to.

~~~

If we would listen to our kids, we'd find that they are largely self-explanatory.

~~~

Nothing ensures that kids will misbehave like regarding everything they do as misbehavior.

~~~

Dry, Sly and Wry

By the time kids acquire the ability to reason, they have become fully acquainted with the advantages of not doing so.

~~~

No kid enters his or her teen years with a well-thought-out exit strategy.

~~~

By the time you understand a 14-year-old, he turns 15.

~~~

Whether you think a kid likes you or hates you depends pretty much on your interpretation of blank looks.

~~~

It is difficult to understand kids, for their minds are undeveloped while ours are still undeveloping.

~~~

Learning

Keynote Thought

If there's one thing I know for sure, but, alas, there isn't.

~~~

Observations

Learning is a lifetime process, but at some point you have to stop adding and start updating.

~~~

If I had it to do again, I would ask more questions and interrupt fewer answers.

~~~

You only stop getting wiser when there is nothing left to learn too late.

~~~

*The mind has this in common with the body --
that it needs a regular bowel movement.*

~~~

*It's amazing what you can learn by listening to
people you don't want to hear it from.*

~~~

*Between the things you learn to live with and
the things you learn to live without, you can
learn to be pretty unhappy,*

~~~

*Looking back, you realize that everything would
have explained itself if you had only stopped
interrupting.*

~~~

*The hardest thing about becoming
knowledgeable is that you have to give up
certainty.*

~~~

*If you keep rephrasing the question, it gradually
becomes the answer.*

~~~

Life

Why be saddled with this thing called life expectancy? Of what relevance to an individual is such a statistic? Am I to concern myself with an allotment of days I never had and was never promised? Must I check off each day of my life as if I am subtracting from this imaginary hoard? No, on the contrary, I will add each day of my life to my treasure of days lived. And with each day, my treasure will grow, not diminish.

~~~

<u>Observations</u>

*What to do with your one life? The same thing
you would do if you had two lives and this were
the second.*

~~~

*As you wait for better days, don't forget to enjoy
today, in case they've already started.*

~~~

*We have a choice every day -- to act on
yesterday's good intentions or get an early start
on tomorrow's regrets.*

~~~

*You have a claim on life, and at some point life
will offer you a settlement. Don't take it.*

~~~

*There are people who live their whole lives on
the default settings, never realizing you can
customize.*

~~~

Life

No matter how you rush about, you discover at the end of the day that you traveled at the speed of time.

~~~

You can awaken each day to obligations you never chose, or you can decide today to choose them.

~~~

A happy life is always complicated.

~~~

Life is short, God's way of encouraging a bit of focus.

~~~

There is always a new chapter in life. You ride into the sunset and discover it's the sunrise.

~~~

You don't want to get to the end of life's journey and discover that you never left the interstate.

~~~

The more side roads you stop to explore, the less likely that life will pass you by.

~~~

*God sends the dawn
That we might see
The might-have-beens
That still might be.*

~~~

You only get one life, but you can't get through it as only one person.

~~~

If you don't decide what your life is about, it defaults to what you spend your days doing.

~~~

There is a purpose to our lives that each day tugs at our sleeve as an annoying distraction.

~~~

Life is not fair, nor has it ever been, but the morning seems determined to dawn until it is.

~~~

Life

You can live your life so as never to rock the boat, but you could have done that by not being born.

~~~

Why does life give you nothing when you ask for so little? That's why.

~~~

Life is not about discovering our talent. It's about pushing our talent to the limit and discovering our genius.

~~~

What a snapshot is to your life, your life is to eternity, so wouldn't it be nice if eternity captured you smiling?

~~~

At day's end, Mother Nature has just one question for us, "What life did you nurture today?"

~~~

Life is all about discovering things that do matter in the end.

If You Want My Advice

Never say never, and never, ever, say never ever.

~~~

Never be surprised if what must inevitably happen happens right now.

~~~

How True, How True

Sometimes your life seems like a furniture arrangement where everything is exactly where you told the delivery guy to leave it for now.

~~~

Things happen in everyday life that make you consider living your life just every other day.

~~~

Life never tires of testing the proposition that life must go on.

~~~

Speaking For Myself

I want to thank God for my life, which is to say,
for this brief opportunity to explain myself.

~~~

I've learned this about the graceful exits you
make in life -- they are 10% grace and 90% exit.

~~~

I count myself lucky, having long ago won a
lottery paid to me in seven sunrises a week for
life.

~~~

I don't so much regret the road not taken as my
all-fired hurry along the road I took.

~~~

I've discovered that you don't have to be a movie
star to live a less-than-glamorous offscreen life.

~~~

Truth is, I haven't hit that many homeruns in
my life, but, then, I never had a steroid era.

~~~

I think my life would make a great TV movie. It even has the part where they say, "Stand by. We are experiencing temporary difficulties."

~~~

This I know -- if they ever do my life story, it'll run on weekday afternoons.

~~~

Do I rue a life wasted doing crosswords? Yes, but I do know the three-letter word for regret.

~~~

Just when I think I've lost all interest in life, I lose a coin in a vending machine.

~~~

Long ago I decided that If I ever get a second life, I will be beautiful and clever and rich -- and that has allowed me to focus on this life.

~~~

Oh, what I would give to relive my life with a one minute delay.

~~~

Life Is...

Life is a series of stages, each preparation for
the previous.

~~~

Life is a grand party where no one gets to meet
the host or stay to the end.

~~~

Life is a vale of tears in which sometimes you
just can't stop giggling.

~~~

Life is like sailing. You can use any wind to go
in any direction.

~~~

Life is a brief opportunity to do something
prehumously.

~~~

Life is like a kumquat -- you kumquat do this,
and you kumquat do that.

~~~

Create Your Own Aphorism

When you get right down to it, only three things are necessary in life -- faith, family and an occasional [select].

Selections:

cold beer
cup of tea
walk in the woods
day at the beach
shopping spree
pepperoni pizza
your choice

Loneliness

Keynote Thought

Nightfall, and the lonely crowd disperses to become lonely separately.

~~~

Observations

In the end, who among us does not choose to be a little less right to be a little less lonely?

~~~

Perhaps we misjudge other people's loneliness because we are so seldom with them when they're alone.

~~~

It is a good friend who respects your solitude but won't let your loneliness have a moment alone.

~~~

If God had intended us to be alone, there would be more pleasure in massaging our own shoulders.

~~~

There are lonely days, when the mind recalls promises not kept, and lonely nights, when the heart recalls promises not made.

~~~

Speaking For Myself

In my loneliest dream, I am alone on a station platform, having missed the last train to eternity.

~~~

Line From An Unfinished Novel

"She lived alone, kept company by a dog that never barked and a phone that never rang."

~~~

Love

Keynote Thought

We never give up wanting things for ourselves, but there comes a day when what we want for ourselves is someone else's happiness.

~~~

Observations

You know you've found love when you can't find your way back.

~~~

It's love when the world stands still, and it's you who are spinning on your axis.

~~~

When the very sight of someone makes you an optimist, it's probably love.

~~~

We picture love as heart-shaped because we do not know the shape of the soul

~~~

It is not necessary to be strong in every place if in the place you are vulnerable, you are loved.

~~~

You know it's true love when reality sets in and it doesn't change a thing.

~~~

Sometimes the shortest distance between two points is a winding path walked arm-in-arm.

~~~

It's true love when you can't think of any way to use it to your advantage.

~~~

Sometimes love is just a comfort in each other's presence that shows up as long silences on the interstate.

~~~

Love

The hardest thing to learn in the game of love is when to fold a winning hand.

~~~

The greatest gift we give to someone who loves us is to just be happy.

~~~

Love never lets you get away with an unspoken lie. It makes you tell it.

~~~

Some say that true love is a mirage. Seek it anyway, for all else is surely desert.

~~~

*Being loved by all is little fun
Unless you're also loved by one.*

~~~

Love is given to us as a time, but to keep it, we must make it a place.

~~~

Once a man has won a woman's love, the love is his forever. He can only lose the woman.

~~~

It is a curious merit system that love observes, rewarding us for just being who we are.

~~~

If you could be the perfect person your lover imagines, what would be the point of love?

~~~

There is more love at second glance than at first sight.

~~~

It is not given to the human heart to love less in order to love equally.

~~~

In the eyes of love we are beautiful, and even more astonishing, we are lovable.

~~~

Love

*Love is not about grand intentions. It is about
small attentions.*

~~~

*No one complains of being a prisoner of love
who has been a prisoner of loneliness.*

~~~

Love is the greatest touch-up artist of all.

~~~

If You Want My Advice

*Before you pledge your undying love to
someone, make them promise they won't die.*

~~~

*While debating the question, "What is love?",
yield to all desperate desires to make someone
happy.*

~~~

See also Marriage, Relationships, Soulmates

Marriage

Marriage is the unforeseen consequence of marrying for love.

~~~

Observations

There comes a time when two people realize that their separate schemes can be better achieved as a conspiracy.

~~~

There is basically just one marriage vow, and that is to be the person someone thinks they're marrying.

~~~

Sometimes a woman marries a man for what he has, and sometimes she marries a man because she is all he has.

~~~

How True, How True

One thing you learn in a long marriage is how many sneezes to wait before saying, "Bless you."

~~~

Love is blind, but it isn't deaf. It can turn plainness into beauty, but it can't turn snoring into a good night's sleep.

~~~

Speaking For Myself

The older I get, the less time I want to spend with the part of the human race that didn't marry me.

~~~

I don't know that a marriage was ever made in heaven, but I know that heaven has been made in a marriage.

~~~

Dry, Sly and Wry

The wedding is where two become one. The marriage is where they decide which one.

~~~

The reason that everyone's smiling in wedding photos is that it's based on the information they had at the time.

~~~

We all play the leading role in our own life story, except for a married man, who plays the husband.

~~~

Words To Remember:

"Each for the other and two against the world."

~~~

Memories

Keynote Thought

Nostalgia is not so much the memory of better times as of higher hopes.

~~~

Observations

There are memories that will always make you lonesome but will never make you sad.

~~~

The happiest memories are of moments that ended when they should have.

~~~

When you look back on the happy times in your life, what strikes you is how flimsy the excuses were.

~~~

Speaking For Myself

There are memories I choose not to live with,
but we hang out at the same bar.

~~~

I am grateful for all memories, so much of my
life having escaped my attention altogether.

~~~

One thing I clearly overestimated was the
number of things indelibly stamped on my
memory.

~~~

Under every full moon,
I recall a lagoon
Where a mandolin played,
And memories stir
Of the dreamers we were
And the plans that we made.

~~~

Mom

Keynote Thought

If you have a mom, there is nowhere you are likely to go where a prayer has not already been.

~~~

Observations

Eventually you realize that the reason God didn't always answer your prayers is that He was answering your mom's prayers.

~~~

Through both their lives, a mom never stops chasing her child down to the water's edge.

~~~

There is little you achieve whose possibility was not first exaggerated by your mom.

~~~

There seems, early in life, to be countless reasons for happiness, and then you discover your mom is making them up.

~~~

A mother always counts to ten,
And never, never peeks,
But always knows just where you hide.
And there she never seeks,
Until the very nick of time,
Lest tears run down your cheeks.

~~~

Conscience is less an inner voice than the memory of a mother's glance.

~~~

Sometimes, in a moral struggle, we remember a lesson our mother taught us, just as on a cold winter's day long ago, we discovered mittens pinned to our coat sleeves.

~~~

If loving you less would make you happy, do you suppose your mom wouldn't try?

~~~

Mom

All I know about life is that it was the first thing my mom ever volunteered me for.

~~~

Every woman knows how to play the single mom, and does so exactly to the extent her marriage requires.

~~~

Overheard: "The best friend I ever had was not trying to be my friend, she was trying to be my dad."

~~~

Eventually you realize that your mom knows exactly who you are and has been trying to break it to you gently all your life.

~~~

All we ask of mom is to rejoice when we find someone who can make us happier than she can.

~~~

How True, How True

A mother forgives you all your faults, not to mention one or two you don't even have.

~~~

A mom reads you like a book, and wherever she goes, people read you like a glowing book review.

~~~

A mom sees past your excuses to the real reason it's not your fault.

~~~

Speaking For Myself

The words of my first confession, "I disobeyed my mother," would suffice for every sin I have committed since.

~~~

I guess I have never doubted that we are all born to our guardian angel.

~~~

Morality

Keynote Thought

It is not easy, the choice between God and the devil, for it is presented to us as a choice between forgiveness and understanding.

~~~

Observations

What you need to know about the offer Satan made to Christ in the desert is that He makes it to everybody.

~~~

As a general guideline, it's good to avoid actions that would be lying and cheating if somebody else did them.

~~~

You must question a code of ethics that never impedes your progress.

It is not known whether God has created a heaven for the good-intentioned, but He probably intends to.

~~~

Evil has this advantage over good -- that it always acts on its intentions.

~~~

Most people plan to get to heaven by faith or forgiveness, which leaves a small niche opportunity for someone following the Ten Commandments.

~~~

Speaking For Myself

I am less motivated by people urging me to do the right thing than by people assuming that I will.

~~~

All I ask of anyone who would judge my sins is that they consider the sins I was capable of.

~~~

Opportunity

Keynote Thought

Opportunity is a parade. No sooner does one chance pass than the next is a fife and drum in the distance.

~~~

Observations

If I were Opportunity, I wouldn't just knock, you'd have to sign.

~~~

Seize every opportunity along the way, for how sad it would be if the road you chose became the road not taken.

~~~

As you seek new opportunity, keep in mind that the sun does not usually reappear on the horizon where last seen.

Optimism

Keynote Thought

The optimist doesn't know whether life is a comedy or a tragedy -- he's just tickled silly to be in the play.

~~~

Observations

The average pencil is seven inches long with just a half-inch eraser, in case you thought optimism was dead.

~~~

How many times must the sun rise before a pessimist realizes it's going to keep doing it.

~~~

How do you tell an optimist that he or she has lived a happy life by mistake.

~~~

*The way to dispel negative thoughts is to insist
that they have a purpose.*

~~~

*To be a pessimist in this world is to sit by a
stream of golden nuggets and pan for sludge.*

~~~

*God created an endless day with intervals of
light and darkness. It is the optimist who
created tomorrow.*

~~~

Define Optimist

*An optimist is someone who thinks that taking a
step backward after taking a step forward is not
a disaster, it's a cha-cha.*

~~~

*An optimist is someone who figures if it walks
like a duck and quacks like a duck, it's the
bluebird of happiness.*

~~~

Parenting

There is no scientific theory of the universe that sufficiently answers the question, "Who entrusted to me this child?"

~~~

Observations

When you bring up kids, there are memories you store directly in your tear ducts.

~~~

A parent's love is whole no matter how many times divided.

~~~

Parenting is a stage of life's journey where the milestones come about every fifty feet.

~~~

The first thing you learn as new parents is why the maternity ward was working on three shifts.

~~~

What you must accept as a parent is that you can't always be there for your child without sometimes ruining everything.

~~~

Parenthood is the passing of a baton, followed by a lifelong disagreement as to who dropped it.

~~~

Anything we tell our kids about life is a placemarker until they figure it out for themselves.

~~~

It is one thing to show your child the way, and a harder thing to then stand out of it.

~~~

The trouble with learning to parent on the job is that your child is the teacher.

~~~

As parents we guide by our unspoken example. It is only when we're talking to them that our kids aren't listening.

~~~

Do not ask that your kids live up to your expectations. Let your kids be who they are, and your expectations will be in breathless pursuit.

~~~

The trouble with having a stubbornness contest with your kids is that they have your stubbornness gene.

~~~

The clash between child and adult is never so stubborn as when the child in us confronts the adult in our child.

~~~

You can regard your child's every reaction as a referendum on your parenting, but it sure is asking a lot of a kid.

~~~

Parenting

If life is theater, parenting is improv.

~~~

There are days as a parent when you would feel trapped and overwhelmed if it weren't so beside the point.

~~~

One thing about parenting is the flexible hours, which can be any arrangement totaling 24/7.

~~~

It is only when we have a child we cannot love enough that we understand why our parents loved us too much

~~~

There are days when you'd just like to enter the world of your child's imagination and never return.

~~~

In the happiest of our childhood memories, our parents were happy, too.

~~~

If You Want My Advice

If you teach your kids nothing else, teach them the Golden Rule and "righty-tighty, lefty-loosey."

~~~

Speaking For Myself

In a dark moment, I ask, "How can anyone bring a child into this world?" And the answer rings clear, "Because there is no other world, and because the child has no other way into it."

~~~

I say to my child, "I will explain to you as much as I can about life, but you must understand that there is a part of life for which you are the explanation."

~~~

How, child, do I know where you're headed? Because I'm there, and I can see you coming.

~~~

Dry , Sly and Wry

All any child needs is the protection of loving parents and an alternative source of information.

~~~

You try to raise kids who are secure in your love and certain of their next meal, which, let's face it, doesn't leave you a whole lot of leverage.

~~~

The parent-child relationship is unique in that the parent does all the favors and the child carries all the IOUs.

~~~

Parenting is an amateur activity that requires professional cleaning.

~~~

See Childhood, Kids

Passage

Keynote Thought

When I am gone, my love, do not look for me in the places we used to go to together. Look for me in the places we always planned to go to together.

~~~

When Death Comes For Us

When death comes for us,
may our lives be already safely stored away
in the minds and hearts and memories of those
we have loved,
and in the happiness and well-being of all we
have helped,
and may death find no life to take from us
but shuffle off defeated,
having relieved us only of our dying.

~~~

Perseverance

Keynote Thought

How often in life we complete a task that was beyond the capability of the person we were when we started it.

~~~

Observations

A river never beats its head against obstacles. It always goes around, and it always gets to the sea.

~~~

Making a different mistake every day is not only acceptable, it is the definition of progress.

~~~

Two things are needed to succeed -- a sensible plan and a willingness to stick to it when any sensible person would quit.

~~~

The trick to playing second fiddle is to play it like second Stradivarius.

~~~

*A nod,
a bow
and a tip of the lid
to the person who
coulda
and shoulda
and did!*

~~~

As a means to success, perseverance has this advantage over talent, that it does not have to be recognized by others.

~~~

Genius is a plodding intellect, incapable of dreaming up the obstacles that stop the rest of us.

~~~

We lack resolve and blame fate, mistaking the drift for the tides.

~~~

You start making progress in life when you realize that you don't always have to resume where you left off.

~~~

If You Want My Advice

Never demand, never beg. Be like a river seeking the sea -- politely insist.

~~~

Stubbornly persist, and you will find that the limits of your stubbornness go well beyond the stubbornness of your limits.

~~~

When you feel down on your luck, check the level of your effort.

~~~

See also Adversity, Success

Personality

Keynote Thought

A winning personality is not just getting people to like you but getting them to like themselves when you're around.

~~~

Observations

People judge you by first impression. The better your first impression of them, the better they judge you.

~~~

Personality is not just saying hello, but dropping whatever you're doing to say hello.

~~~

Charisma, personality -- there are lots of labels for the knack of always giving people your full attention.

~~~

Dry, Sly and Wry

Remember, if you had the friendliest, most winning personality in the world, you'd always wonder if people liked you just for your personality.

~~~

Speaking For Myself

I have this knack of making people feel good about themselves -- not so much charisma, I think, as comparison.

~~~

Pets

It is a special friend who dispels your loneliness but leaves your solitude intact.

~~~

Observations

A friend we allow into our company, a pet we allow into our solitude.

~~~

Life is mostly a good reason to go for a walk with your dog.

~~~

The difference between a dog and a person is that when you earn a dog's love, you get it.

~~~

There is no better actor than a dog pretending to be as sad and lonely as you are.

~~~

It is almost unbearable, the look in a dog's eyes that says, "I would gladly be your soulmate, if I only had a soul."

~~~

If animals could talk, the world would lose its best listeners.

~~~

A cat, after being scolded, goes about its business. A dog slinks off into a corner and pretends to be doing a serious self-reappraisal.

~~~

Ever wonder where you'd end up if you took your dog for a walk and never once pulled back on the leash?

~~~

An old dog, even more than an old spouse, always feels like doing what you feel like doing.

~~~

Our pets know that they are loved less than our children, but, alas, they have no sense that their need is less.

~~~

At some point in life, you discover that nothing is fun forever, which news you then have to break to your dog.

~~~

The most important lesson we learn from our dog is to kick a few blades of grass over it and move on.

~~~

Speaking For Myself

I am accused of favoring dogs over people when, in fact, I favor whoever comes running when I whistle.

~~~

I had a good day with my pets -- my dog came running to greet me, and I have a 2:30 appointment with my cat.

~~~

Pets

I don't suppose my dog has human feelings, but he sure lets you know when you hurt his instincts.

~~~

I am not your dog, but if every time you saw me, you gave me a backrub, I'd come running to greet you, too.

~~~

My dog and I have enjoyed many a silence together, a conversation always resumed exactly where left off.

~~~

On the whole, I would not wish to live a dog's life, except for the times when you show up to help and are told to go lie down.

~~~

I have concluded that my pets feel guilt, although perhaps not nagging guilt.

~~~

Dry, Sly and Wry

*No dog is fully committed to the proposition
that it doesn't bite.*

~~~

*Psychologists now recognize that the need to
own ten cats is really a sublimated desire to
own twenty cats.*

~~~

*In a world of doors, the inability to open a door
can be mistaken for a desire to lie underneath
the dining room table.*

~~~

*You tell something to your dog, who tells
another dog, who tells another, and it can be
hilarious the way it comes out.*

~~~

See also Animals

Politics

Keynote Thought

No matter what the political system, its aim is always its own preservation, and its means is always you.

~~~

How True, How True

The difference between science and politics is that science experiments on guinea pigs.

~~~

When a politician tells you that we're all in this together, you can be pretty sure you weren't in it before.

~~~

The first rule of politics is, "Never explain, and do so at length."

~~~

One hears little common sense spoken in politics, due to the risk of alienating its opponents.

~~~

There is scarcely one of the Ten Commandments that, if acted on in concert, would not be a plot to overthrow the government.

~~~

You can fool some of the people all of the time, also known as a base constituency.

~~~

Politicians follow a simple rule: Deny it, and if proof turns up, deny you denied it.

~~~

Every political candidate has an economic policy that will reduce the taxes of the people he's talking to.

~~~

What you find in a democracy is that it's hard to build a house when every nail has an opinion.

~~~

Dry, Sly and Wry

Politicians don't lie, they misspeak, and they don't steal, they mispocket.

~~~

Washington D.C. classified : "Unaffiliated hack seeks party."

~~~

Wouldn't it be great if voting for someone didn't have to be an act of forgiveness?

~~~

There are Seven Deadly Sins, of which, so far, only Envy and Greed have organized politically.

~~~

The difference between a politician and a pickpocket -- but there I go again, splitting hairs.

~~~

In fairness, not all politicians leave office richer than when they went in. Some are still in office.

~~~

Politicians are divided between those who cannot resist temptation and those who no longer require it.

~~~

The hope in a two-party system is that the 2+2=3 party and the 2+2=5 party will work out a compromise.

~~~

The difference between embarking on a political career and embarking on a criminal career is the formal announcement.

~~~

Overheard in a Washington D.C. confessional: "Bless me, Father, for sins have been committed.

~~~

Possessions

Keynote Thought

What a treasure are the things we have learned to live without, for no thief can take them from us.

~~~

Observations

Anything we possess that is not necessary for life or happiness becomes a burden, and not a day goes by that we don't add to it.

~~~

We realize we can't have everything, and so begins the mad dash to have everything else.

~~~

I am never five minutes into removing the clutter from my life than I start running into the clutter that is my life.

~~~

The best things in life are not only free, they require less assembly.

~~~

There are more lines formed than things worth waiting for.

~~~

Dry, Sly and Wry

I had this nightmare the other night where a burglar broke in and left stuff.

~~~

I don't know that people with lots of possessions are happier, but they sure put on better yard sales.

~~~

Thought at a yard sale: "Whoever said that something is better than nothing seriously underestimated nothing."

~~~

Reality

<u>Keynote Thought</u>

*Question reality, especially if it contradicts the
evidence of your hopes and dreams.*

~~~

<u>Observations</u>

*The realist sees reality as concrete. The optimist
sees reality as clay.*

~~~

*Some, fearing reality, retreat into their
imagination, but most, fearing their
imagination, retreat into reality.*

~~~

*Perception is a clash of mind and eye, the eye
believing what it sees, the mind seeing what it
believes.*

~~~

There is a relentless tendency of things to become what they seem.

~~~

In the realist you have the sorry sight of the five senses deprived of their imagination.

~~~

The hardest thing about reality is returning to it after an hour inside your child's mind.

~~~

<u>Speaking For Myself</u>

If I choose abstraction over reality, it is because I consider it the lesser chaos.

~~~

*If the world existed
But in my invention
Wouldn't it pay me
More attention?*

~~~

Reality

I have learned over the years that my eyes can construct a figment as easily as my imagination.

Dry, Sly and Wry

To accept reality is only to encourage it.

~~~

One may accept reality without necessarily accepting the current arrangement.

~~~

There is a difference between denying reality and avoiding it whenever possible.

~~~

Perhaps the Lord gives us a physical body so that when we change our minds, we won't be somebody else.

~~~

Relationships

*If you go to bed happy in your relationships,
what matters the hassle of the day?*

~~~

Observations

*A relationship is never perfect, which is why it is
so important that it be loving.*

~~~

*The best relationship is the one that gets you to
like the person at your end of it.*

~~~

*In a lasting relationship, you have two people
who can't think of anything that was not part of
the deal.*

~~~

Relationships

We all know the part of ourselves that needs to be harnessed. It takes someone else to know the part that needs to be set free.

~~~

Once you find someone to share your ups and downs, downs are almost as good as ups.

~~~

There are days when you need someone who just wants to be your sunshine and not the air you breathe.

~~~

As important as shared memories is the silent agreement that certain things never happened.

~~~

To truly know someone is to know the silence that stands for the thing they never speak of.

~~~

When two people like the same music and the same movies, they can usually work out differences in politics and religion.

~~~

As a rule of thumb, never leave a relationship while it's still important to you that the other person understand why.

~~~

Sometimes, in a relationship, we blow things out of proportion because proportion is so dull.

~~~

There are times when two people need to put on the brave face they show to the world and show it to each other.

~~~

A loving relationship can become fun, but it's a better bet that a fun relationship will become love.

~~~

Many a relationship would be improved by one more degree of separation.

~~~

There comes a point in a relationship when you realize that you trust someone enough to let them keep their secrets.

We are, many of us, a planet orbiting somebody's sun, unconscious of a lonely moon, orbiting our planet.

~~~

In the best partnerships, one dreams dreams and the other dreams financing.

~~~

Things happen in a relationship you need to forget, and if you don't think so, congratulations, you forgot.

~~~

Speaking For Myself

I have found that winning isn't everything, and, in fact, in the relationships I most care about, it isn't anything.

~~~

See also Growing Apart, Love, Soulmates

Retirement

Keynote Thought

Retirement is having nothing to do and something always keeping you from it.

~~~

Dry, Sly and Wry

Retirement is a period in life when people can talk your ear off without wasting a bit of your time.

~~~

One question that comes up in retirement is what to do when a police officer tells you to go about your business.

~~~

It's a consolation to know that the person you might have been would today also be retired and playing golf.

~~~

Retirement

It is hard to love the human race when you only meet people in traffic.

~~~

A good thing to do in retirement is to check occasionally to see if your brain is rotting away. For example, did you recently buy life insurance at "only $6.95 a unit."

~~~

See also Aging

Sanity

To be sane is to know that there are parts of the mind that you cannot enter with any hope of returning.

~~~

Observations

Sane or insane, we are all multiple personalities, sanity being the ability to settle on one spokesperson.

~~~

Among creatures born into chaos, a majority will imagine an order, a minority will question the order, and the rest will be pronounced insane.

~~~

Dry, Sly and Wry

The problem with a severe delusional state is that it attracts followers.

~~~

The paranoid thinks that sinister forces are out to get him, not realizing that they are out to get everybody.

~~~

Insanity is doing the same thing over and over again, expecting a raise.

~~~

Despite the goings-on in Congress, I don't think the U.S. is bordering on madness. I think Canada and Mexico are.

~~~

Speaking For Myself

Though I've never been certified insane, I continue to earn credits on my equivalency.

~~~

Self-Esteem

Dry, Sly and Wry

Oh, what we might accomplish, were it not for an exaggerated sense of our own unimportance.

~~~

Observations

Lend, by your imperfections, self-esteem to others, and you will be invited everywhere.

~~~

If we could see others as they see themselves, our shyness would soon become compassion.

~~~

Before you discourage a child, consider what damage to your childhood self-esteem you now believe was temporary.

~~~

*Be thoughtful of others and you will not be shy,
for they are incompatible addictions.*

~~~

*Until you confess your sins publicly, you have
no idea how much people don't care.*

~~~

Dry, Sly and Wry

*Nothing contributes to self-esteem like having a
loving partner, perfect kids and a seriously-
flawed best friend.*

~~~

*Test your self-esteem: If you were the last
person on earth, would you be beautiful, ugly or
of average good looks?*

~~~

*Nothing boosts self-esteem like discovering a
really cool soulmate.*

~~~

Self-Interest

*You do not wake up one morning a bad person.
It happens by a thousand tiny surrenders of
self-respect to self-interest.*

~~~

Observations

*What you must realize about self-interest is that
it loves to pose as your better judgment.*

~~~

*The trouble with selfish motives is that they
start to look like principles, and you end up
sending your kids to die for them.*

~~~

*One's conscience should never be apprised of
one's property holdings.*

~~~

Siblings

Keynote Thought

There is a bond forged between two people who have hid together under the same bed.

~~~

Observations

The advantage of growing up with siblings is that you become very good at fractions.

~~~

There is a strong chance that siblings who turn out well were hassled by the same parents.

~~~

A toast once heard: "To my big sister, who never found her second Easter egg until I'd found my first."

~~~

See also Family

Solitude

I enjoy both company and solitude, and in the company of my solitude, I find both.

~~~

Observations

There are times when you seek your solitude, and your solitude just wants to be left alone.

~~~

I have always needed a place to go to as refuge from the crowd -- and a crowd to go to as refuge from that place.

~~~

What a blessing to be alone with your thoughts when so many are alone with their inability to think.

~~~

Solitude

No matter how reclusive we tend to be, we picture the afterlife as a community of souls. It is one thing to seek privacy in this life; it is another to face eternity alone.

~~~

Speaking For Myself

There are times when I'm alone with my thoughts, which is to say, not alone enough.

~~~

Forsaking my friends, I sought my solitude, only to discover that my solitude preferred my friends.

~~~

Dry, Sly and Wry

Sometimes people think you're cold and aloof when you're just aloof.

~~~

Soulmates

Keynote Thought

There doesn't have to be anyone who understands you. There just has to be someone who wants to.

~~~

Observations

You will not find a soulmate in the quiet of your room. You must go to a noisy place and look in the quiet corners.

~~~

One day, in your search for happiness, you find a partner by your side, and you realize that your happiness has come to help you search.

~~~

Eventually soulmates meet, for they have the same hiding place.

~~~

Soulmates

When something is missing in our lives, it usually turns out to be someone.

~~~

What we find in a soulmate is not something wild to tame but something wild to run with.

~~~

Eventually, if you're lucky in life, you find someone with the same chemical imbalance you have.

~~~

You list all the reasons why no one could ever love you, and then one day you meet someone with the same list.

~~~

Sometimes, I think, we are allowed to get lost that we might find the right person to ask directions of.

~~~

Having perfected our disguise, we spend our lives searching for someone we don't fool.

~~~

In a soulmate we find not company but a completed solitude.

~~~

There are few greater joys than having a dream you cannot let go of and a partner who would never ask you to.

~~~

To find someone who will love you for no reason, and to shower that person with reasons, that is the ultimate happiness.

~~~

*"He was a sad and lonesome clown,
And she was the circus that came to town."*

~~~

See also Love, Marriage,Relationships

Success

The road to success is not a path you find but a trail you blaze.

~~~

<u>Observations</u>

Try to discover
The road to success,
And you'll seek but never find,
But work to succeed,
And the road to success
Will trail right behind.

~~~

The first requirement of success is to show up.
The second is to make it clear you're not leaving.

~~~

Success is a tale of obstacles overcome, and for
every obstacle overcome, an excuse not used.

~~~

Every partial failure is a partial success, so if you haven't succeeded, maybe you haven't had enough partial failures.

~~~

So often we are kept from our goal not by obstacles but by a clear path to a lesser goal.

~~

Success is not about who you know. It's about you know who.

~~~

One key to success is to have lunch at the time of day most people have breakfast.

~~~

Few on the road to success get past the exit to social acceptance.

~~~

You embark on the road to success when you stop dreaming dreams and start dreaming plans.

~~~

The surest sign that the goal is near
Is that offers of help begin to appear.

~~~

It's always good to admit when you've failed, by
way of establishing who gets to decide.

~~~

You know you're succeeding when the people
telling you it can't be done start changing their
reasons.

~~~

The road to success is wherever people need
another road.

~~~

Dry, Sly and Wry

No matter what you achieve in life, your friends
will chalk it up to luck and your relatives to the
grace of God.

~~~

See also Adversity, Perseverance

Time

Keynote Thought

*Time is a figure eight, at its center the city of
Deja Vu.*

~~~

Observations

*There are three dimensions of time, two of
which contain better days.*

~~~

*First God created time. Then God created man
that man might, in the course of time, perfect
himself. Then God decided that He'd better
create eternity.*

~~~

*Time brings an end to everything, often
mistaken for a tragedy.*

~~~

Time

For centuries, man believed that the sun revolves around the earth. Centuries later, he still thinks that time moves clockwise.

Speaking For Myself

I have never wished for more hours in the day. There are already more than I have time for.

~~~

I suspect that time is to eternity what a waterspout is to the ocean -- a brief disturbance on its surface.

~~~

I live on a tiny planet orbiting a minor star. Each time the planet completes an orbit, I count off a segment of my life. Why do I do it? I dunno, it passes the time.

~~~

I have found that time heals everything, unless skin-related.

~~~

Tolerance

Keynote Thought

I look into the faces of people struggling with their own lives, and I do not see strangers.

~~~

Observations

You wonder why those of us created by God can't just get along with those of us whose ancestors crawled out of the sea.

~~~

Speaking For Myself

There are many alternative life styles that would offend me if they were any of my business.

~~~

Tolerance

Rather than seeing it as traffic, see it as thousands of individuals determined to give it another day.

~~~

Bear no ill will that you have not pondered beneath a starry sky, or on a canyon overlook, or to the lapping of waves and the mewing of a distant gull.

~~~

<u>Speaking For Myself</u>

I have never understood the purpose of hate, or how you know the purpose has been accomplished and you can stop.

~~~

Truth and Lies

*To deny any truth is to begin a chain of denial
that must eventually deny every truth there is.*

~~~

Observations

*Two things are owed to truthfulness -- lasting
marriages and short friendships.*

~~~

*The first step toward telling the truth is to tell
the whole lie.*

~~~

*Worse than telling a lie is spending the rest of
your life staying true to a lie.*

~~~

Every lie has a reason, the reason also a lie.

~~~

Sometimes a person may lie to you only once, just as sometimes your house may be infested by only one termite.

~~~

Every lie is two lies -- the lie we tell others and the lie we tell ourselves to justify it.

~~~

If there be no God, then what is truth but the average of all lies.

~~~

If You Want My Advice

When you speak, always tell the truth, but don't always speak.

~~~

Wealth

Keynote Thought

Wealth and wisdom are seldom combined, for the person who achieves one no longer desires the other.

~~~

Observations

Measure wealth not by the money you have but by the things you have for which you would not take money.

~~~

The problem with spending your life seeking wealth is that you never get wealthy enough to buy back your life.

~~~

It is an assumption of the rich that those who are happy with little will be happier with less.

~~~

Youthful idealism is the belief that the portion of our parents' wealth not being used to put us through college should be distributed among the needy of the world.

~~~

Dry, Sly and Wry

It doesn't seem fair that a greedy few should have all the wealth when the rest of us are just as greedy.

~~~

Money always ends up in the hands of the rich, first going through a money-laundering operation called the economy.

~~~

Everyone favors the redistribution of wealth, the wealthy favoring the way it's already been redistributed.

~~~

There is less wealth than there are fair shares.

~~~

~~~

Appendix

~~~

Leftovers

If you can't explain it in a few words, try fewer.

~~~

Less is owed to courage than to the mistaken belief that there's nothing to be afraid of.

~~~

There is a logical explanation for everything, often mistaken for the reason it happened.

~~~

It finally happened -- a lawsuit for wrongful doing unto others as you would have them do unto you.

~~~

It's not a stupid question if it gets a stupid answer.

~~~

I have never heard the words, "There is no easy way to tell you this," without thinking afterwards that there was an easier way.

~~~

Listening to some folks expound, it's clear that not everything they swallow is chewed thirty-two times.

~~~

People are resilient. After all, every person born has recovered from nine months on life support.

~~~

In sinners and repenters, you have the original division of labor.

~~~

Massage is the only form of physical pleasure to which nature forgot to attach consequences.

~~~

It's reported that three out of four small businesses fail, a definite argument for starting a large business.

~~~

Leftovers

Well, it finally happened -- a first class stamp is too valuable to risk sending through the mail.

~~~

Is it my imagination, or does shipping and handling settle a box of crackers more than it used to?

~~~

IRS: an agency patterned after the revenue-raising concepts of the 19th-century economist, Jesse James.

~~~

Words from the past: "It's a clever idea, Mr. Bell, but don't wire us, we'll wire you."

~~~

Nowadays you envy a manic-depressive. Half the time he's happy, the other half he's right.

~~~

I have never met anyone who wanted to save the world without my financial support.

~~~

*As to the Seven Deadly Sins, I deplore pride,
wrath, lust, envy and greed. Gluttony and sloth
I pretty much plan my day around.*

~~~

*You can spend too much time wondering which
of identical twins is the more alike.*

~~~

*How do you know when enough is enough?
Hint: enough is always enough.*

~~~

*Inscribed on a cave dweller's wall: "They who
do not know history are condemned to start it."*

~~~

*Always telling the truth is no doubt better than
always lying but equally pathological.*

~~~

*I look at it this way, I'm not an eavesdropper; I
have an attention-surplus disorder.*

~~~

Signs And Posters

On the interstate: "Fines Doubled Next 30 Miles. Various Reasons."

~~~

Bumper sticker: "My Son Is An Honor Student At Ed's Online University."

~~~

Billboard: "Just Ahead. Acme Smell-The-Roses-Drive-Thru."

~~~

On the interstate: "Speed Monitored By Low-Flying Humming Birds."

~~~

Bumper sticker: "I Brake For Flashing Blue Lights."

~~~

Billboard: "Clyde's Honing Pigeons. Knives, Cutlery Sharpened."

~~~

Bumper Sticker: "Turn Signal Not A Guarantee Of Future Performance."

~~~

On the interstate: "Leaving Work Zone. Resume Speeding."

~~~

Billboard: "Visit Our Secluded Island Paradise. Flights Every Hour."

~~~

On the interstate: "Traffic Slows Ahead. Nobody Knows Why."

~~~

30980149R00123

Made in the USA
Charleston, SC
01 July 2014